Welcome to
"Pictures of Big Black Cocks"

Inside, you'll find funny pictures of majestic black cockerels!

If you're in need of a giggle, this book will have you squawking with laughter.

So get ready to crack a smile and enjoy the feathered fun!

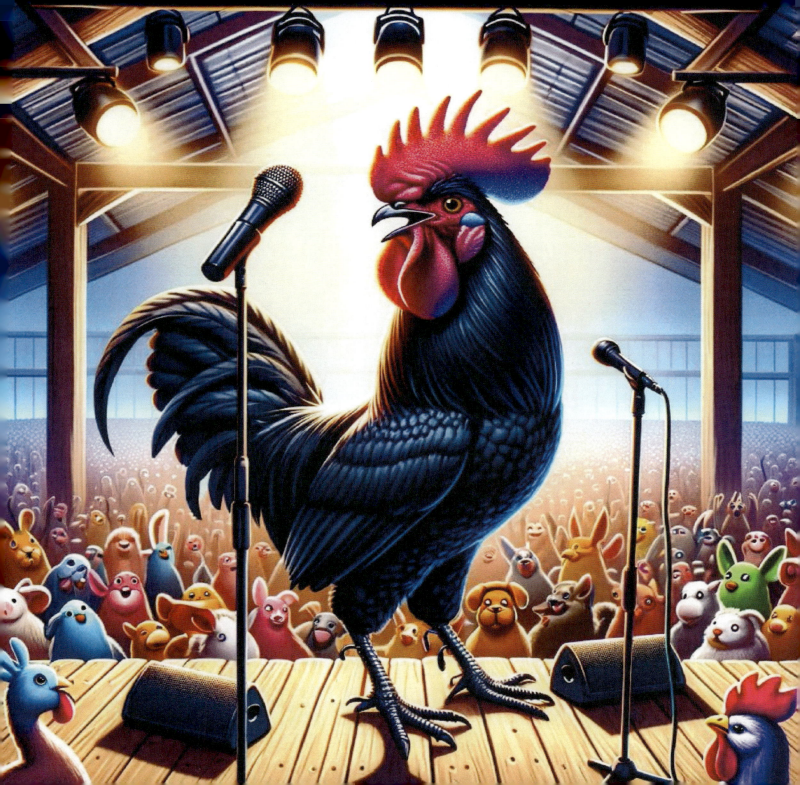

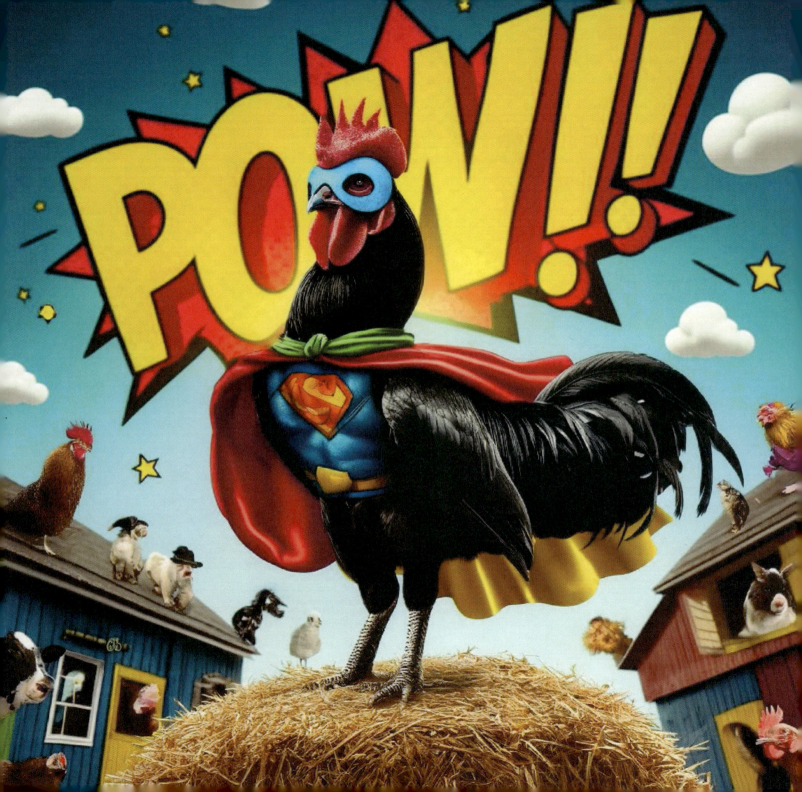

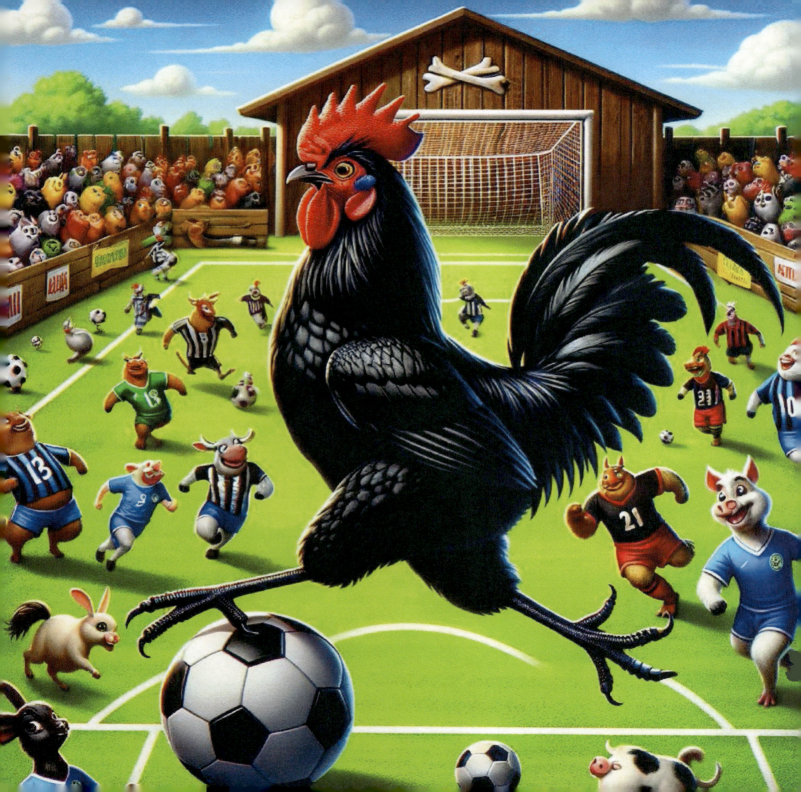

Printed in Great Britain
by Amazon